SKOOKUM RAVEN

SKOOKUM RAVEN

HEATHER HALEY

Ekstasis Editions

Copyright © Heather Haley 2020
Cover art: Derek von Essen

Published in 2020 by:
Ekstasis Editions Canada Ltd.
Box 8474, Main Postal Outlet
Victoria, B.C. V8W 3S1

Ekstasis Editions
Box 571
Banff, Alberta T1L 1E3

All rights reserved. No part of this book may be reproduced in any form without the written permission of the publisher, with the exception of brief passages in reviews. Any request for photocopying or other reproduction of any part of this book should be directed in writing to the publisher or to ACCESS: The Canadian Copyright Licensing Agency, One Yonge Street, Suite 800, Toronto, Ontario, Canada, M5E 1E5.

LIBRARY AND ARCHIVES CANADA CATALOGUING IN PUBLICATION

Title: Skookum raven / Heather Haley.
Names: Haley, Heather, author.
Description: Poems.
Identifiers: Canadiana (print) 20200225960 | Canadiana (ebook) 20200226010 | ISBN 9781771713900
  (softcover) | ISBN 9781771713917 (ebook)
Classification: LCC PS8565.A4328 S56 2020 | DDC C811/.6—dc23

Canada Council for the Arts   Conseil des Arts du Canada   Funded by the Government of Canada   Canada

Ekstasis Editions acknowledges financial support for the publication of *Skookum Raven* from the government of Canada through the Canada Book Fund and the Canada Council for the Arts, and from the Province of British Columbia through the Book Publishing Tax Credit.

Printed and bound in Canada.

For my tricksters

Contents

Piratical

Dawning Consciousness	13
A Larcenous Groom's Cool-Off Period	15
Rookie	17
Moll	18
Seeker	19
Queen of Eggs	20
Rock Star	21
Pseudocommando	22
Monster Lost	23
Hug Deprived	24
The Expat	25
The Lapsed Catholic Does Not Confess	26
Praise	27
Manhunt	29
The Humble Muralist and the Reproachful Buddhist	30
Field Trip	32
Insomnia	33
How To Dodge Limbo	34
Sop Recovery	35
Visiting Hours	36
Tempo	37
Houla	38

Skookum Raven

Bird Watching	41
Mama	42
Hard Times	43
One Dress	44
Shroom Hunt	45
The Junco Does Not Reflect	47
Insomnia Redux	48

Pacific Time	49
Flux	50
Retreat	51
Torrent	52

Ripe to Stray

Voracious	55
Mirage	57
Our Thirst	58
Volcano Watch	58
Mission	60
Door Man	61
Top Floor	62
Beauty Sleeping	63
Wares	64
Dorothy Undressed	65
Hood Point	66
Near Fatal Interruption	67
Single Handed	68
Winter Heat	69
Every Hand Job	70
I Saw You	71

Clown Duty

My Week	75
Rough Cut	76
Upstart	77
Ghost Pilot	78
Terminal Labour	79
Clown Duty	81
Distractions	82
September	83
Dirty Work	84

Detective Work

Charm Offensive	87
Motoarsonist	89
Immune	90
Suits	91
Riots of Pussy	92
Detective Work	93
escape artist	94
Hans	95
Extinction	96
Rude Awakening	97
Flesh Pot	98
Wild West/Coast	99
The Last Ping	100
ACKNOWLEDGEMENTS	103

PIRATICAL

Dawning Consciousness

She wakes grimly febrile,
desperately nostalgic
to dawdle in ditches
of tadpoles,
to wager glass
marbles in snow lanes,
sew mini-skirts
for her Barbie,
for mashed potatoes,
fried baloney,
the gag reflex.

She shuts her eyes,
snubs the town's lens
zooming in on her culpability.
Incensed at the sun's insolence
she rises despite collisions and
the most recent death toll.

She groans, engulfed in tokens
of admirers, embattled by and
dreading the delirium of desire,
one lover resolutely phlegmatic
as the other effuses and plummets.
No incidental leaf
but a loose lunatic rook,
mate in the old-school canon.

Men ostensibly, on,
off or side-tracked,
their interpersonals interpenetrate
their fictions, demands and tousles
so delightfully incessant.

No accident this transport back
to forsaken tracks,
giant drainpipe.
I engineer it.
I, of humble origin,
melancholic disposition
provide stimulation and
orchestrate robberies.

I, in the cliché of a crisp white shirt
and black hat
inflict pain, increase pressure,
draw hostility, reel in crisis
commonly referred to
as authentic experience.

I dare to sprawl,
invite expansion
as vital to my vitals
as blood on needlework.

A Larcenous Groom's Cool-Off Period

He filches tunes: fuck copyright.
Downloads steamy nude pics,
provides a market, not Paypal.

He pilfers
pop for his hottie Charlotte,
slots 'em in the fridge door,
stacks 'em in the pantry,
enough Coke to fuel a militia.

He boosts
street signs. That'll stop their goddamned
touch-the-sky routine,
bestows his buddy Guy
with a JACKSON ST,
a little vainglory for the double-wide.

He lifts
century-old chairs,
stuffed wildlife
from a leaning farmhouse.
Ed the Fence thanks him for the laugh:
"Now get the fuck outta here."

He pinches
his sister-in-law Emily
in the pocketbook.
Emily, who mourns the loss
of her younger sibling.
"I'd like to hearse her away
for Chrissakes."

But he gives. He gives!
To the church,
indirectly, every time he mows
Our Lady of Sorrows' lawn:
"Cos they ain't paying me enough
to do this shit
and it's fuckin' hot as hell out here."

Rookie

Fleeting night,
Windows eternally flicker
With reality show glimpses.

Headless psyches,
A fleck of remembrance.
My brief childhood.

Dumb, young adulthood.
Grim hospital stay of a marriage.
My next of kin reside in the past.

I plod like a donkey.
55 and I need more
Time. Miles. Cash.

Born harried, will I die a novice?

Moll

Home away from home
To maul his favourite barfly,
The one who's heard it all.
Meek dick-taker. Instant co-spiralee.

No-guff companion quickly enamored
By her salient recycled mate.
Faithful ego extension, she waits
Patiently, fourth in line.

It's a reckless man
Who underestimates her pale grip,
Courts the highly functioning
Simpering angel face, dressed up

To impersonate a pure silk purse.
He orders a beer. "Have a cup of cyanide,"
Says the innkeeper, "it goes down quicker
And delivers a more merciful fate."

Seeker

She found him
Verbose, wondered
Why he gargled,
Carved salt with his uvula.

Too much tongue?
She was the type
To fondle Q- tips
And groom his climax—

Swish. Swallow. Marvel.
The questioning type,
Blessed or cursed
With a savant-prone womb.

She found his northern slums
More frightening than marsh,
Collarless dogs
Or red grapes

Frozen in the sun.
She found me
Long after she'd quit
Seeking answers, clarity, peace.

Queen of Eggs

Exit ovary
Stage left
One of two million
Accidents.

Raised on peril
Raised on nothing
But the back of her hand.
By puberty

She'd crushed the stars
Bowled the moon
Over and plowed our Plymouth
Into the crest of Mt. Robson.

Horse-playing coquette, she
Charmed beauty salon gal pals
Bus station grandpas
Jukebox addicts

And shuffleboard kings
Out of their winnings
While morning raids on
The landlord's cluckers

Ensured we never ran out.

Rock Star
For Dave Gregg

Head of fur.
Unabashed depth charging
Renegade,
Wilderness as alive inside him
As a cascading river,
Night a badge
Over his savannah heart.
Heroic trickster
Dutifully howls,
Scatters stars coyote-like,
Unerringly sharing his light.

Pseudocommando

Cave of an apartment.
Lonesome injustice collector,
Lame Prospero,
He maintains relations
With others based on envy,
Writes romances of revenge.

Between mean-street patrols
And bitch prowling, he corrals
The unwanted, hated, feared bits
Of himself to reassemble in
The form of an enemy
Who deserves merciless rage.

Monster Lost

Godzilla years
Vagabond phase
Rampage days
Punch & Judy show
Nights. Wild west
Pastiche. Bang
Locals. Streamline fate.

No coastline suits,
No dwelling
Can contain him.
Latent crush
She did not choose.
He fell into her
Living room

Woozy from flight.
Parsimonious talker,
Familiar, fragile giant
Pockmarked with luck.
Collisions. Pain.
She did choose to look.
To see. To harbour.

Hug Deprived

Oxytocin starved paramour
Mimics Orion,
Hunts scorpions,
Chases skirt
Up the wrong leg.

The inability to secrete,
Let down, feel empathy;
Hence the psycho prevails.
Clashes resound.

Squelched desires jangle.
Jilted road-trip astronaut
Double-parks her diaper
To pepper spray a rival

While back on earth
Nothing blows up well
For the demolitionist,
Neither concrete miscreation
Nor deteriorating bridge.

The Expat
For Russel Wills

The un-American, though
Part of him never left.
Fully himself. Always.
Flinty

As the black starlings fighting
For food in the snow.
Imprisoned he abides
Alongside the milk cows,

Returns to his cache of sky,
Sun-skin and kinetic clouds
Each night, each night a starlit carriage,
Buffer between long sighs and
Dawn's troughs of slop.

He spurns downhill arrangements,
Damning sentences,
Fading graffito,
The blank, gruff strumpet's voice
In favour of any, of all women.

Envisioning, he
Raises a ladder to the window,
To a view of summer,
To life as he knew it.

The Lapsed Catholic Does Not Confess

In February Ma's temper
Steams the window.
A flutter of wrens alight,
Plying the bare-limbed willow
As if it's a lyre.
Fawn, dove, hare
Shelter in cedar shade
Still and frightened.

Bonded in blarney
She raised me
On clever jive,
My conception a farce,
Life a fiction.
Let the need to know go
She repeated, as if she knew Buddha.

Her demise should illuminate
Every secret, every corner,
Every cowering tot
Lit by the pop and flash of
Truth, triumphant at last.

Praise

Blonde brick facade
Fails to deter local rapture consultant,
Friendly neighborhood ecstatic man
Gleeful with belief.
Brother Earl pronounces

That each defeat of the heart,
Each leave-taking
Must ignite a torch song for Jesus.
Any definition containing the word "God"
Is proof of God, according to Earl.

She protests, demurely.
He persists, naturally.
There is no convincing the devout
You don't need convincing.
The righteous crave victory
More than fishes and loaves,
She, his undeserved indulgence.

Piqued, he spends days
Mane taming,
Malignifying
Every utterance
Out of her reluctant mouth,
Discourse so acute
She threw up her hand.
A signal.
STOP.
Let's restart.
Imagine peace.

Expert at diminution,
He named her Heathen. Sub-human.
Steeply ignorant. Condemned.
Though the pious never cease flaming
Both remain sanguine. Standing.

Manhunt

The Colonel defiantly birdlimes.
Favours an icebox.
Clotheslines. Sideburns.

He nobbles me at every party.
Blunderbuss, star philosopher
Flip flopping across the sand

To opine. Flap, flirt.
Surf my turbulence.
Overweening egghead,

Three armholes required.
He descends to my level
To parse, probe, fix

My diabolical lump. Such
Easy-to-spot men. Easy
to track. Easy to lose.

The Humble Muralist and the Reproachful Buddhist

Island roads are only as long as the island,
invariably leading to the vortex every island hosts,
the village or burg hugging the cove or bay,
the place where sweaty, unrepentant
cokeheads and alcoholics
wind up, gurgle down, to rub
elbows with the vigorous and Tilley-hatted,
swamping the gentry
with their nasty habit stench.

Island roads rove lowly
through swaying grasses, expansive elms,
past lambs, cows, horses, llamas
But do not be lulled.
Anxiety stalks the dales and hollows,
tamped down, concealed behind neat
rustic wooden fences,
skulking in the cottages
despite a glut of acupuncture outlets,
yoga, meditation and pottery classes.
Here there is much intestinal discomfort,
ceaseless aspiring, straining
toward the light.

Dolly for example is the biggest Buddhist
bad black sheep
herder on Paisley Island,
happily bending over
for regular shearing
as long as the taxman
is tranquil about it
and she's back at the ranch in time
to inject herself
into the tête-à-têtes.

Her resident good egg Greg studies
the recommended sutras,
working on his anger,
moving past it, out
of his townie flat to create
murals in the great outdoors.

Grandiose depictions,
towering *trompe l'oeils*.
Ostentatious? Yes,
but they have provided
our meek hamlet with an angle,
a tourist attraction.
Indeed, they sustain us.

Field Trip

Take umbrage.
Sour all I have.
Do not rock kismet,
Delight in peals of spring.
Mired, I flicker, follow
A waif; wily, poisonous, we
Pervert high school rituals,

Claw hammer rivals,
Blind to the nests,
Cocoons, hives, shells,
Snoozing in biology class,
Oblivious to organisms
Living in, on, through us.
All escape our attention.

I know I must
Observe, take notes.
Name stars and species,
Salvage withered specimens,
Friends. Repair things
Beyond repair.
Sail toward a ship.

Insomnia

She sips her black tar fizz
Remembering
Batik, macramé, totems,
A beaver upon a plinth.

As sturdy and useful
As a shorthorn bull
She prefers to reside
In her head and wonder,
Who will thwart the meteorites,

Who will save the future?
Rain pelts the window,
Mothra softly dying
To reach lamplight,
To deliver sleep.

How To Dodge Limbo

She's a before photo.
A fossil, suspended
In amber, on display. Perfect
Example of what not to do
When you know not what to do.

She's a limp hill-headed escapist,
Maiden in name only.
She took his offer,
Got his goatee but not intent
To trample and renege.

Do not wait
For the next move.
To lurk is to infest.
Do not descend into minutiae.
Do not kill

Time. Do not wait
For the after-photo. Perfection.
Do not wait. Do not
Do nothing.
There is no glory in limbo.

Sop Recovery

Mangled post tequila,
Narcotic of estrangement,
But up from the basement,
Pretty feet restored,

I propel myself
With nothing
But will,
Grateful for the veil

Of mist, of icy piano note
Raindrops. They strafe
What's left
Post hacking

Into,
Hacking away.
Hmph.
He's not the only martyr

Dragging me down,
Blowing me up.
I will sleep in mud,
In a river,

A harridan
Sharper than thistle.
Embraced,
Sheltered, cleansed.

Visiting Hours

Conk.
The allure of punishment.
No reason to be here
Yet here you are,

Fist curled round
A morphine pump.
Gonna grow a pair
Or remain dented for life?

Your brain child and butter
Wielding wife arrive.
The smiling know
What's important,

Though forced like you
To fabricate hazards,
Harness weather,
Feign injury.

Tempo

Pulse forgotten,
A player piano tears
Through tunes.

Violet eyed Diana
Fingers a book, her alphabet
Soup just as hot outside.

Secret fondled, tendrils ironed,
She chooses the painted door,
Each stair whistling in time.

Houla

An infant is not a toy.
An infant cannot breathe underwater
Or fly though the air. Do not drape it
Over the prone man's head

Or dress it up like a doll.
Journalists view the grisly scene.
Post. Share. Tweet.
UN observers abort,

Prominent commentators punt.
But the drunken skipper acts,
Ordering clean sheets and neat rows
Down below in the hold.

Rogue unidentified man
Hoists the limp boy
Aloft.
Let's not quibble.

It matters not if the child
Is southern or northern,
Whined or knew pride.
It's as good as dead.

Crooked passages.
Limping messengers.
Frantic, dog-chasing-tail orbits.
A million ships cannot transport us.

SKOOKUM RAVEN

Bird Watching

Binoculars resting on the sill
Blackly inveigle us to look.
The luxury of observation,
Rackety silk.
Cotton sheets abuzz,
I sleep with a mad bomber
In a bed too narrow
To contain explosives.
Eroding acres encroach
Shores of receding flesh.
Grip off, I watch

Elfin hummers amok,
Flap-happy mallards
Swarm a blustery afternoon.
I recall bionic gunrunners, East Van,
First day back from gangster land.
Recoiling at the forecast I'd fled,
Cramped in a compact car,
A woman piloting the wife at last.
Blindfolded against his scrutiny,
Foiling implicit shame, I skirted
*Road*blocks, sculpted my spine
Straight, forced it
To withstand gales. Tolls.

Lousy steward, I drop
The argillite raven,
Gleaming abalone eyes divided.
I slap my back with hot plasters
So it might bend when necessary.
Fit inside. Repair.
When will listening
Reveal the shape? When
Will seeing decode the trick?

Mama

Beefy titmice.
Permanent chickadees.
Cubs, cute
Marvels I must leave,
Push, fling, provide
The briefest infancy.

Hard Times

Fathers must frown
On all that flags or is soft,
On sentiment and church-dodging,
On dummies.

Dad disapproves of alone moments
No matter how hard it gets.
Extend yourself, Numb Nuts
And you will be rewarded with stature.

Mama also frets the fluids,
Alpha Pop declaring:
No stains. No beach. Align yourself
With your brothers. Mask nothing,

Abide. Or I'll give you something
To cry about. I'll inflict the day.
Bumps. Loads. Crowing cocks.
Substance. A crossroad or two.

One Dress

Collection dress,
Worn
To harvest clams,
To fish in,
Open-ended.

Pink, floral,
One dress
Lures salmon
To the river's mouth.

One dress
To do it all,
Our genes stalking
Her salty nest.

Shroom Hunt
For Julie V

High life burns.
Rainforest beacons.
Blue stains. A spread of teeth.
Rotting wood, dung, conceal
Earth tongues. Fleshy to waxy,
Roundish to lumpy.
Puffballs.

Carbon Cushion.
Ustulina deusta
Easily detached.
Bump like. Rolling spore.
Elfin speaker shies away,
Courting lively buttons.

Fairy Ring.
Marasmius oreades
In grass. Good, with caution.
Predator bird alerted.
One eye open.
Scarlett shagged. Bone tortured.
Adapted to a rattle of stars.

Pretty Phaeocollybia.
Phaeocollybia fallax
Radishy. Under Sitka.
Flustered. Melodious.
Moss biography.
Trap door to dream state
Open.

Reddening Lepioata.
Lepiota americana
Free gills. Smooth. Bruised.
Partial veil, morals cultivated
In the pit of a honeycombed head.
Nothing frivolous about the search.
Still, velvety mischief abounds.

The Junco Does Not Reflect

Bonk. Window sabotages
Flight path.

Poor sparrow.
Despite this map of a face

I get lost in a blink,
Find no one in the mirror.

Oh, my pulp-fiction life's
Been a diary of woe.

Rhythm partner left me
Nothing but sorry joy,

Entirely enervated.
His remaining thugs say

My stunned-bird routine is
Hyperbole. Who to believe?

Insomnia Redux

Cypress Mountain beams
Singe my bed,
Illuminate dread.

The island glows
As if a tropical
Sun sets in strata
Of violet, longing
As brief and crushed
As a single-winged heron.

Pacific Time

Cedar jungle.
Left coast.
Mellifluous bees and

Hummingbirds swarm
The morning, a teeming creek
Bows to the sea.

Chocolate hens and hares
Consume the household
Quickly. Mugs stacked,

We steep and fuse.
Volatile lives lampooned.
Bursts. Snipes. Rants

Compelling as a drowning cow,
Pert hustler rising in your skull.
But see, Howe Sound

Currents obviate
Previous episodes, ancient
Grievances, low levels.

Forget restitution.
Leave the old scow
To rot on the alluvial plains.

Flux

Sundogs melt.
Tuna tins expire.
Honeybees purge,
Headless sea lions wash up

And bloat. Hydrangeas drown.
Squirrels retreat.
Vacant towering firs
Hush the songbirds

Via gust. Ravens squawk.
Telecom tricksters call
And call. And call.
Carbon copied dread

Routed to the periphery,
Mt Galiano a distant lump.
Inviolate taint in the mainstream.
Traveling vast distances

My blood recedes,
Limbs tread water.
Garnering muscle,
Mustering will and

Cranking tunes, I summon
A glint of valour,
A smidgen of honour,
Then dive.

Retreat

Red cedar raven roost,
A feat invisible as its roots,
Heavy metal imbued groundwater
Purified through sheer will.

These trees that breathe
As I pant. Sigh. Wish
I could tell you.
Branches sway, camouflage

My fatal bent, freckles. Green canopy
Conceals skewed moments, missed cues,
Taint, our silence lulling as a zephyr,
Our blindness sweet as sheep.

Torrent

The blooms of August,
Barren foxglove.
Last island summer
Set ablaze. I bolt,
Sloppy spy mission complete.

Deadheads snag crossing.
Buffers hinder streaming
But ruin is fluid,
Handily lifting my kayak,

Absconding with the ice.
Linen skin burned, I traverse
The swollen moat,
No salve nor catharsis
Upon reaching the far bank.

RIPE TO STRAY

Voracious

A kiss.
Coral. Incandescent.
We wanted a kiss.
We wanted a moment
of no one knows us.

In a hovel or the firs
we wanted a moment
of no one watching.
We wanted a ride,
the roiling innards.

We wanted a night.
One night, to escape
the ether, the library,
all that shushing.
We wanted more
than one season
of abundance.

We have entered text
red as a target,
invited a stoning,
but we are very bear.
Mewling accomplice
pawing at the door,
I track charred meat
from bower to suite.

From a fly coastal trip
drenched in dark highway,
through a fuming winter
of snarling heat,
to blasted spring robins
and lilacs blaring perfume,
we have muzzled nothing,
growling in the gut wicked
as songs loud as our heads,
deafening aches
silent as screen voices
deep at night.

Mirage

I strive to wake slowly
To answers, to morning
When I hear best
When I am best heard.

Oh, what's my weather?
Clammy Kurt Cobain
In my decapitation dreams.
The verdant commotion.
The microchip dread.

Don't shy away,
Don't pretend you can't see
What you see.
Here comes your tall order,

Last Coke in the desert, he
Whom you'd thought out loud,
Sacrifice-bunted and
Bent light rays for
Is made manifest. Integral
Part of the landscape.

In dubious collusion
With my dawdling beau
Inspirational quotes
Make me puke,

The unsaid so uneasy.
There is no rain.
No water.
No lake.

Our Thirst

He's a towering, pensive Danny Boy,
Bloodied. Unbowed.
She's a lithe, simmering
Scar-brandishing tomboy.

Preeminent cursers,
Junkyard-dog hearts, they
Swap reflections
And damage.

Kiss us. We're Irish. Black Irish.
We invented melancholy, we
Lap up sea squalls like puddle water,
Nip tragedy in the ass.

We devour angst, roll over despair.
We brood, pour, grapple, shove. Fight
The good fight and function, dammit,
When called upon.

Big, deliberate, quixotic, plodding
Through calamity. Breathing little,
We flail against ourselves,
Rail, smack, filch each other's bones,

Laugh in the morning.
Done with grief.
Catholic as we may be
Do not go down. Know Hell. Knees.

Swells. Rise again and again
Through the slag and the flames,
The bellowing waves.

Volcano Watch

Punch tools. Cutups.
Antlered animals.
Arm bones astonish.
Antipodes hook.

Winged jewels.
Bluegrass blades.
Amaranthine throats.
Nothing lost on me.

I am tossed about
In a volcano man,
Billows of black
Tidings. Lured to the horizon

Through a corn maze,
Past turbulence of mind,
Nothing but pink
Stars to separate us.

Mission

Graves loom,
The nasty is sequestered.
I hear your hulk
Shading the cliff.

Logic lemming-leapt,
We weave a net of arms,
Invent a shepherd,
Exhaust satiety.

We couple courage,
Shoo dimwits,
Estimate fallout.
You plead neutrality,

I plead soldier brain.
We are not happy
Until the cottage is razed,
The harvest ploughed asunder.

Door Man

New pain. Old pain.
Everything hurts.
You never leave,
Chief wound.

In our kitchen universe
Knockout incidents morph
Into one gorgeous fight.
I sanctify slaughter,

Swine my pearls so well.
You hire me to steal,
To father your tribe,
Whitewash collisions

And do what's required.
Resplendent in martyr guise
You're beyond reproach
In glaring red numbers.

Woody fruit burst
In the insensible bed,
Our small house forsook,
For sale. Black corset never worn.

You're sucked on in the green room
For miles and miles,
Another score before grace
As your offspring walk in half.

Top Floor

I was there
But can't recall
A blur.
You are here,

Unsullied.
Wet towers sway.
I admire the dirty gulls.
You land

On the top floor,
Move the mirror, ceiling,
Unhinge the doors,
Make no mistake,

Persist in limbo,
Leaving me
Soaked, juiceless, waiting.
You, above it all.

Beauty Sleeping

In our household era,
That hidden decade
Of robust and tidy children,
Our souls ripped and rubbed
And became guarded.
Hard blessings, hard blessings.
I remember building bees,

Libido in limbo,
Brutal cakes,
Stove anchor,
Frenzied scrubbing,
Simmering war,
Derelict lips,
My eyes flying open.

Wares

I need a good barrel. Or barrelful.
Beer, rain, oil, doesn't matter,
Just give it to me
Then go

Or come, oh nuisance caller
With nothing to sell and less to share.
Will we ever buy into one another?
Exchange crowns? Silence crickets,

Respective niggles?
'Tis folly, seeking sanctuary
Beneath a bat-roosting tree.
Their jaunty black-sky scribbles

Invade our periphery,
Jolt our creaky alliance.
Cold in front of the fire,
Burning side by side,

Stones skip beyond us, the
Cinema of sunset so banal
It provides no sidetrack.
Score. Or anything we want.

Dorothy Undressed

When I, as in a dream
Am not me
I am free.
A sudden jerk

May stoke the cold
Stove but when I
As in a dream
Am not me

I am free to divest
Gingham pinafores and
Flying sock monkeys.
When you, always you

Find me at last
It might be too late.
Posture all you want
My rangy munchkin

It is too late
To smoothe cotton things out.
The house is abandoned,
Hot iron inside.

Hood Point
Dec 31, 2012

Lost in stars
Brave as ash
Wrestling shadows
Giddy with night
I lure water taxis to shore
Light the oven
Salt the path
So I may reach you
Cliffside,
Burnish your gleam.

Nearly content on our
Last night, last supper
We spot blue herons,
Our whooping over.
Lashings, lamb bones,
Bent-finger pointing,
Steam building, hot
Boxing, fur ball
Hangovers, bellicose
Stroking, done.

News wrapped as fish.
Jesus-hair obscures horns
Of sunny fog-ferries,
Our flight from one another
After twelve days of
Balancing hurt.
Out with the year
Of tedious brinkmanship.
No end to the apocalypse jokes,
Lucky 13, new affirmation.

Near Fatal Interruption

Pond forsook, shed tippled,
I seek gusto, the jolly,
Adroitly avoiding east, his
Brilliant mean declarations,
Confabulations,
Sorry offensives.
Our fractured liaison.

The work of forgetting
Sickens, my Saturday night
Lacerated by a trip to the ER.
Belligerent patients triaged;
Inebriated Cosmo girl car crash,
A severed digit,
Meth-addled troll.
"My heart is quitting!"
Your erection won't.
Happy to see me.

X rays, blood work
Reveal nothing
But our deficits.

Single Handed

Strays, yard rats, we
Share a national railway,
An urge
For burning corn,
A penchant for
Leaving each other
Tied to the tracks
In the depths of night.

Creosote-smeared legs
Stand in a deep cove
Now, manning my boat.
Trip charted,
Lovers never quit
Beckoning, inserting
Keys, truncating
My swagger,
Saving me
From this lonely perch,
This vast wave.

Winter Heat

You and I. We
Warm the cabin
With a fiesta.
Slow dances.
Torturous torch songs.

I favour kiosk chocolate,
Cormorants black as cinder.
He who orchestrates touch,
Who once handed me
My limping orders,
Favours things melted.

You ban air quotes and kink.
Me, fake railings and balloon releases,
Especially for no occasion.
You inform me that yes
Some gingers are cold.
I confide that meanly handsome
Hot-headed micks
Only make me think of we.

Every Hand Job

Every hand job
Ever given
Every hand job
Ever received
Belongs to me.

Every furtive grope,
Every stolen kiss, mine.
You fuck
I come.

The time you delivered pizza
To a silk-robed widow, the one
Who relieved you of your virginity,
I was there.
That was me.

I've been inside
Every bachelor apartment
In the world
Since bachelors began.

Your escapades, my escapades.
Your sex, my sex.
I lick, suck, bang for you
Whenever you can't come.

I Saw You

Girl reading a book.
Long yellow scarf.
Big black SUV.
Grace on wheels.
Born a ginger, I could tell.
Crushing!
Psych night.
Passing in the rain.
Dark hood and jeans.
Cursing myself,
Should have got your number.
Seated next to me at the hockey game
We shared popcorn and a Kinder Surprise.
Foggy falls at Seymour, rode the chair together.
Tattooed blonde on the bus to Horseshoe Bay.
Criminal. I like you. A lot.
Teacher in Surrey, living in Van.
You had a giant bottle for making mead.
Whistler Gondola Saturday morning,
Still embarrassed by my runny nose.
You asked if I knew of any liquor stores open
Past six on Sunday night.
Hottie tequila boy
Working the front desk.
Skytrain to downtown
With your soil erosion papers,
So gorgeous
I couldn't get up the nerve.
Cowboy in white hat driving white Corvette.
Yaletown brew pub smiles.
Mountain biking. Tennis court. Pit bull.
Sunset Beach @ Sunset.
I saw you.
Red Bull poolside party.
Liked your glasses.

Davie Street block party.
Screaming for ice cream.
Rent cheque. Rex I am obsessed.
Fairmont Pacific Rim lounge late last night.
Hypnotic regression.
Coffee cutie.
Instantly attracted to your energy.
We came very close.

CLOWN DUTY

My Week

Fed a germ.
Dog tottered.
Spooned flies out of yogurt.
Dislodged ants from the toaster.
Entered words.
Fought for blackberries
And free stuff.

Doctored bites.
Signed language.
Collected greens,
Heirloom tomatoes.
Parsed a meme.
Registered my feelings.

The last house on Husband Rd
Has prolific bamboo décor.
You can sit in a resin chair there,
The white ones especially war-strong.
It's too late in the week
To do anything nice

Or nicely.
Too late in our lifespans
For anything,
Though he's still trying
To Xerox his ass,
Moon the earth.

Rough Cut

After 18 months' gestation
and several bouts of incommunicado-ness
she dutifully reports to the clay eater's
rat's nest to defend her lump of art
before he nibbles away all the footage.

She flatters, pretending
his indiscriminate cravings
and grinding teeth
do not wear her down.

Meth-heads don't generate, they spin
scratched vinyl, shoot blankly,
regurgitate turbulence, gnaw
and brew dandelion wine
because it's free,
free as roadside blackberries
or meadows of psilocybin.

Pirate of his own ship-
bachelor-pad bouncy house-
he sleeps in a pocket on the floor,
close to the cache
when he isn't busy
snipping or sniping.

Under the red toque
a mind's eye so muddied
it can see nothing move.
Bloodied images, frames,
shots blur.

Recreate. Rework. Repeat.
Repeat. Repeat. Repeat.
With no recourse, no kind release
she seriously considers murder.

Upstart

Cineaste selfies over brunch.
Four-dollar toast,
Single-origin coffee,
Post-ironic jokes,
Cold, amusingly terrible eggs.

Actually, I like crap, reports Juan,
Nearly as much as fapping
To Kristen Stewart.

Groan we must, our nuggets
Of wisdom lost
On the 19-year old who
Only needs to sell a few batches
Of home-brewed kombucha
In order to retrieve his skateboard
From the pawn shop.

Juan's a gem,
Director in the rough
With a great idea for a movie
And matching Kickstarter campaign.

Ghost Pilot

Am I dead?
This yoke of command.
No turning back.
Navigating soup.
Procedures forsaken.

Rapid roll to the right
Betrays the horizon.
Wish I'd called in sick.
Voices swap, feel up
The ceiling, glow mortal.
No turbulence but peculiar

Buzzing in the cockpit. An
Undoing. Damn prop flies off,
Slices a hole into the fuselage.
Explosive decompression.
Oxygen over. Fume of fog.

Am I dead?
Terror of hypoxia.
I keep my head. Level my wings,
Scroll hardened bush below.
Anglers caught shooting.
Geriatric moose.

Stronger than-ten-acres-of-garlic
Electra crippled, stuck on full throttle.
Hips shaking, about to rip apart.
High tail? Ditch?
Envision a long, northern runway.

Take the thing by the horns,
Steer, brute muscle mustered.
Stabilize this damn fossil.
Second pass. Last chance. Brace.
Kill the engines.
Committed. Hurtling.

Terminal Labour

Murderous pipe snakes
Through the Rockies,
Ripping our century in two.
Calamity stitches together

Rituals and mollifying dances.
Distracted protesters
Ransack a few days off.
Sour fists, sweet mouths,

Boners in the rain.
He recalls her glass tears,
Tongue of flint,
Silent in the station

Shrewd in the bar.
His dunce fat depleted,
Husk nearly ready
For the casket

He works with her
To remove obstructions,
Excavate a trench,
Contour the land.

Clown Duty

Born wrong he got me right,
Celebrates my fanny,
Antics, black mind
For comedy. Gutterized beau
Replete with affection disorder,
Grog blossoms, cauliflower ear
For doggerel. Broken noise.

Bloviating Master of Ceremonies.
Glittered stallions. Elastic pratfalls.
Nothing distracts from my To-Do List:
Test trapeze. Conduct
Gravity. Polish nose.
Flush away

Chimp guano. Marvel
At the mess we've made, beatify
Our slap-happy love,
Bless big-top bounty.
Remember what matters.

Distractions

Dance. Around my keyboard.
Drive. To your cottage.
Rash on pup's belly,

Mud. Smears on your mattress.
Latest turgid update.
Condom count.

Blows to the noggin.
Ex-girlfriend entreaties.
An ultimatum or else.

Sore peepee.
Fake boobs.
Flaming turd on doorstep.

Your problems.

September

Will summer resist fall?
Will I resist

The drama teacher?
His brutish caress,

His sugarless candy.
Perhaps I can learn

Clandestinely.
Get smart.

Slip out.
Or, will restored,

Make it manifest.
'Tis the season

To move.
Pack books.

Leave
Back doors wide open.

Dirty Work

I am your golden jackal. I shine and grin,
I flash the light, forge trails through night
Blooming jasmine, metropolitan serfdom.
I machete weed, tamp down boozy panic.

In the morning you put on the jacket,
Admit the thrills, hips, heat up our cunning.
Get to chopping. Onions, peppers, kindling.
Start the fire. Sweep. Brew the java. Rouse.

We share bacon, scrambled eggs and signal
Amidst tender yanks. Shrieks!
You entice me with new jeans.
A rumpus in the hay.

Ack! Your alarm clock. Smallness restored.
Inner priest rises to free the calves
We toiled to corral.

DETECTIVE WORK

Charm Offensive

Or, booty call gone bad.
It's not funny. It's murky.

Icy thorns of fury
Recede slower than scars.

Sopping with venom,
Vein of mayhem open,

Angel dust of adrenalin
Winged dainty arms,

Amplified might.
To be admired only at night.

Beloved as a mule,
His shame her cargo.

Serial monogamy, serial frustration.
No getting off this ride.

Flexing reserves of vindicated
Muscle, she kicked ass and dragged.

Fuck spadework,
Made the shower his tomb.

Victuals and body rotted
As speculation rose

Till they found the red stench,
Cordial, self-winding businessman

In fetal position, lenses
In the washer, voyeuristic goo.

Water did not silence the apparatus
Nor launder its images.

Truth as obscured
As that Judgment Day in June,

God in the guise of ex-girlfriend, Jesus
Absent through five years of lynch mob.

Motoarsonist

Distorted in stature,
the duke of a wilderness family
winced at the price of fuel
and the carcasses in his wake.

Malicious by accident
depending on which room
the grilling took place in,
by which cop, Good or Bad.

Benevolently slamming,
he braised ugly hams in the sun,
ate a shit sandwich daily at the wheel
of the taxi he drove all over the city.

Nothing can stop a provocateur.
Nothing can stop ignition,
fires set at night
to divert shame.

Detonated plushly,
the flames trebled,
jumped rank,
jumped lakes and roads
to roar into the ocean
to singe mighty creatures
the giant squid, the blue whale.

Immune

Let us skulk,
Spoof,
Touch wood.
Our lark is long overdue

Though rain must intervene
To doctor numbness,
Float the islands,
Drown ticks and cigarette butts.

Let us linger, ponder,
Graph. So much garbage. Deaf
German Shepherd hears malice.
Medicine arrives post-dumpster,
Mercy too late and garbled.

Let us sit and watch. Chart
The tormentor, his poison aim.
Undiagnosed. Diabolical
Sick puppy.

We are immune.
We must imagine
Fear, a wolf at the door
One prick at a time.

Let us stop. Think.
For beatings, stabbings,
A storm of rattling sabers
Remain the healthy status quo.

Suits

Humour him.
Fly laughter in,
raucous as a murder of crows.

Justifiable fall from grace,
justifiable as his birth.
Hungers dictate.

Epic raids. Illustrious career.
Silk suited decades
til burn out sloppy.

Lazy mistakes hasten proof.
Stains appear.
Crown counsel sport coat,

surname a furious noun.
Ton of testimony,
trousers retrieved from a trench.

Slash marks visible.
Neatly creased
he folded.

Gangster reckoning.
Gold cufflinks lost.
Hangmen earn their hoods.

Riots Of Pussy

Shoot the messenger, burn the witch.
Robo nuns, soldiers and cops
Mash heads, mangle blue balaclavas with red.
Police heat works to freeze tongues.

No way to dodge the rain, sluts smoke
Beneath a bellowing chimney.
Head-gear-removed strip show.
Wet. Bare. Shamed. Silent. *Nyet*.

Detective Work

"Only God knows."
Fuck Him. Horny
Marauder. I disarmed
God eons ago.

I've been blessed
With X-ray vision.
All the better to ogle
Your boobs
Though it's motive I see

Glaring through hotbeds
Of rose mallow,
Blaring past foghorns
Of hickory smoke.

Theories sound
As any scientist's,
I uncover proof
You can't bear
To look at.

Bright, beckoning.
Ultramarine.
Nature vs. nurture?
Fuck that. Murderous intent

Seeped into human cells
Eons ago.
Kill To Live,
It's not just a prison tatt.

escape artist

fence invisible
self-inflicted
barbed wire
scarlet wince
time a mere fever
wrath
my ally
my armor,
my will

Hans

Under the bridge a blanket rests,
Knave tapping to a bush beat.
Hearing reproach in birdsong,
Flak in the bending willows

He may see through concrete
But do not call him clairvoyant.
Merely tenacious,
Tenacious as the wildlife

Lured
From the ribbon of road
To flounder
In a vortex of personality.

I paid the toll.
One drop at a time.
Where is my deliverance?
Still you simmer. Still no loosening

Of your grip from our lovely
Long Jane Doe necks.
Incarceration did not free
Nor contemplation illumine.

We are macerated into mash,
Pulp enough for paper. Fusion
Of forms so 21st century, so now,
So damned imperative.

You aren't about to quit
Stalking or preying
So let it leak. Gush
Around your finger in the hole.

Extinction

Warning: first you lose
The teat, then Dad

May skedaddle, disappear
Like snot into a rag,

Like the delicate mastodon
Or cash, not so petty

Once it's gone. Gone,
What he once embodied:

Mensch. Rock. Guide. Kingpin.
He stands though prostrate,

Christ-less, memory-less,
Spit-built homes

Lost, one each decade.
Gone, his buddy, to Kingston,

Five years for manslaughter
Of desire.

He who eschews matrimony
Harbours a friend

That killed a dude
For fucking his wife.

Gone,
The futile urge to procreate.

Rude Awakening

Thunder protests
This dappled grey morning,
Its skyline of baby teeth,
Gush of soldier ants.

Pestilent dream flickers
Will not scatter. They invade
The dismissive e-missives,
Monster blogs, yammering news;

The highwayman who surveilled
A close-to-the-road family,
Blameless kids playing, oblivious
To the uses of duct tape,

Kids who learned
They were too puny to live,
That you can't move a house
Not made of Lego.

Flesh Pot

We are born muscle-bound,
Backboned with maps,
The matrix of our mothers intact,
Into families, slums,

Manors, private
Security firms, institutions.
Piratical or pious
We proliferate. Raw teeth, germs and

Clubfeet do not impede us,
Nor rank, nor garbled speech.
Our struggle, videotaped drama,
Our tumult banal,

Pain prosaic, strife fueling ripeness,
Gauntlets passed through swiftly
Until the day we drop. Nominated,
Cornered, required to wither

Under the gun,
Succumb, for we remain
That tender, precious human
Flesh terminators aim for.

Wild West/Coast

No lotus eaters we
Swelter pepper,
Swig beer and bitch.
Cook up the rent.

barbecue / cauldron
steak / prize
gavel / tenderizer
We grow enormous,

Righteous, meting out
Beach justice from our camp,
Our point. Our peninsula.
With less mitigation

Than an island, its
Star gardens, clarity
Of marine life penetrates
A sound of silent crime.

The Last Ping

After the girl is gone,
long gone, out of character,
statistical, presumed dead,
the Verifying Department
hops to, sniffs out
the revelers, especially
the life of the party,
his liquid engine of beer.
Anyone with information,
to confirm names and addresses,
substantiate stories?
They watch your gestures.
Read your face.

Last seen wearing a blue ski jacket,
white blouse, black jeans.
Phoenix tattoo ascending
from the right hip,
Bright, unintentional dropout,
inadvertently delinquent.
Boyfriend person of interest.
Always. Constable passes the flyer.
Her cell phone may be dead,
last ping traced—pinpointed in fact—
to here. Right here. Last known location.
Right where we're standing.
This town. Your pretty little town.

Fuckin' A.
Check your property,
shallow ditches.
So petite, she takes up little space
in the psyche,
turkey vultures lead us
not to her
but a deer carcass.
Parents pray
to repair the squabbles. Home.
Local kids clam up,
weighting the secret with smoke.

A teenaged girl can forget
she's graduated
the fenced-in yards of childhood
to this vast plain
where condoms provide safety,
sympathy muttered.
She forgot
townies find transcendence in fury,
one vaguely recalling
Eminem shouts,
a catfight in the backyard.
She looked kinda posh,
smashed-herd fumbling,
fawning, pushing.
Over. Under.
Dancing.
Sending her sailing.

Acknowledgements

Earlier versions of some of these poems were published in:

EVENT, Issue 48, June 2019-"Houla" and "Bird Watching"

Canadian Ginger, anthology, edited by Kim Clark and Dawn Marie Kresan, Oolichan Books, 2017-"Winter Heat"

Splice Today, magazine, 2017-"Ghost Pilot"

The Revolving City; 51 Poems and the Stories Behind Them, edited by Wade Compton and Renée Sarojini Saklikar, 2015-"Flesh Pot"

Art Song Lab, 2015. Music by Brian Topp, performed by William George, Corey Hamm-"Our Thirst"

WAX Poetry and Art, No. 6, Sept. 2014, edited by Kirk Ramdath-"Dawning Consciousness", "Motoarson", "Our Thirst", "Voracious"

FORCE Field: 77 Women Poets of British Columbia, edited by Susan Musgrave, Mother Tongue Publishing, 2013-"Voracious"

The Wild Weathers: a gathering of love poems, edited by Ursula Vaira, Leaf Press, 2012-"Voracious"

The Toronto Quarterly, April 2012-"Hans"

My gratitude to the editors.

I am indebted to eagle-eyed Catherine Owen and her invaluable input.

Thank you to Lyle Neff for his exceptional editing and copywriting.

Thanks to Exstasis Editions for their warm support.

About Heather Haley

Poet, novelist and musician Heather Haley pushes boundaries by creatively integrating disciplines, genres and media. She was Poetry Editor for the *LA Weekly* and publisher of the *Edgewise Cafe*, one of Canada's first electronic literary magazines. Haley has produced and directed numerous videopoems, official selections at dozens of international film festivals. Renowned as an engaging performer, she's toured Canada, the U.S and Europe in support of two critically acclaimed AURAL Heather CDs of spoken word song, *Princess Nut* and *Surfing Season*. Her poetry has appeared in *The Antigonish Review, Geist, The Vancouver Review, FORCE Field: Women Poets of British Columbia* (Mother Tongue Press), *Where the Nights are Twice as Long: Love Letters of Canadian Poets* (Goose Lane), *Canadian Ginger* (Oolichan Books), *The Other 23 & a Half Hours* (Wolsak & Wynn), *Wild Weathers; A Gathering of Love Poems* (Leaf Press), *Verse Map of Vancouver* (Anvil Press), *ROCKsalt: Anthology of Contemporary BC Poetry* (Mother Tongue), *Spoken Word Workbook* (Banff Centre Press) and *Alive at the Center: Cascadian Poets from Vancouver, Seattle and Portland* (Ooligan Press). She is the author of poetry collections *Sideways* (Anvil Press), *Three Blocks West of Wonderland, Skookum Raven* (Ekstasis Editions) and debut novel, *The Town Slut's Daughter* (Howe Sound Publishing), currently being adapted to the stage.

www.ingramcontent.com/pod-product-compliance
Lightning Source LLC
Chambersburg PA
CBHW070939080526
44589CB00013B/1565